Partes de
la planta
Plant Parts

¿Por qué las plantas tienen flores?

Why Do Plants Have Flowers?

Celeste Bishop

Traducido por Eida de la Vega

PowerKiDS
press™

New York

Published in 2016 by The Rosen Publishing Group, Inc.
29 East 21st Street, New York, NY 10010

First Edition

Editor: Sarah Machajewski
Book Design: Mickey Harmon

Photo Credits: Cover (flower) Andrekart Photography/Shutterstock.com; cover, p. 1 (logo, frame) Perfect Vectors/Shutterstock.com; cover, pp. 1, 3–4, 7–8, 11–12, 15–16, 19–20, 23–24 (background) djgis/Shutterstock.com; pp. 5, 22 Patrick Foto/Shutterstock.com; p. 6 dookfish/Shutterstock.com; p. 9 Creative Travel Projects/Shutterstock.com; p. 10 Villiers Steyn/Shutterstock.com; p. 13 nineyoii/Shutterstock.com; p. 14 Joe Petersburger/National Geographic/Getty Images; p. 17 Serg64/Shutterstock.com; p. 18 Pairoj Sroygern/Shutterstock.com; p. 21 photka/Shutterstock.com.

Cataloging-in-Publication Data

Bishop, Celeste, author.
 Why do plants have flowers? = ¿Por qué las plantas tienen flores? / Celeste Bishop.
     pages cm. — (Plant parts = Partes de la planta)
Parallel title: Partes de la planta
In English and Spanish.
Includes index.
ISBN 978-1-5081-4739-8 (library binding)
1. Flowers—Juvenile literature. 2. Pollen—Juvenile literature. 3. Seeds—Juvenile literature. I. Title.
QK653.B57 2016
575.6—dc23

Manufactured in the United States of America

CPSIA Compliance Information: Batch #BW16PK: For Further Information contact Rosen Publishing, New York, New York at 1-800-237-9932

Contenido / Contents

- -

Las plantas tienen diferentes partes. Cada una tiene su propia función.

Plants have many different parts. They each have a job to do.

Las flores son una parte importante. Ayudan a que nazcan nuevas plantas.

Flowers are an important part. They help make new plants.

Las flores tienen **pétalos**. Los pétalos tienen bonitos colores. También tienen un olor fuerte.

Flowers have **petals**. Petals have pretty colors. They also have a strong smell.

pétalos / petals

9

10

Los pétalos protegen el interior
de una flor.

Petals keep the inside
of a flower safe.

El **polen** se fabrica dentro de la flor. Es un polvo amarillo que ayuda a que nazcan nuevas plantas.

Pollen is made inside a flower. It's a yellow dust that helps make new plants.

polen / pollen

13

El polen tiene que viajar de una flor a otra. ¿Cómo sucede esto?

Pollen has to travel from one flower to another. How does this happen?

Las abejas y otros insectos llevan el polen de flor en flor. Los animales, las personas y el viento también lo transportan.

Bees and bugs carry pollen between flowers. Animals, people, and the wind carry it, too.

Cuando el polen llega a una flor, ésta empieza a producir **semillas**.

When pollen reaches a flower, it can start making **seeds**.

De las semillas crecen
nuevas plantas.

Seeds are used to grow
new plants.

21

¡Las flores son muy importantes!
Sin ellas, no tendríamos plantas.

Flowers are very important!
Without them, we wouldn't
have plants.

PALABRAS QUE DEBES APRENDER / WORDS TO KNOW

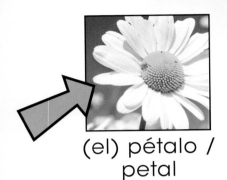

(el) pétalo /
petal

(el) polen /
pollen

(la) semilla /
seed

ÍNDICE / INDEX

SITIOS DE INTERNET / WEBSITES

Due to the changing nature of Internet links, PowerKids Press has developed an online list of websites related to the subject of this book. This site is updated regularly. Please use this link to access the list: www.powerkidslinks.com/part/flow